Wicked Christianity
All Rights Reserved by the Author

If you would like to contact the author, please do so through
wickedchristianitybook@gmail.com
http://www.gbtministries.com

All references are from the King James Version

Wicked Christianity

Written by

E. C. Graham

Table of Contents

Wicked Christianity

Wicked Christianity

Good and Evil

Wicked Christianity

Since the day that Adam took the fruit of the tree of knowledge, man has been engaged in deciding what is good and what is evil. The natural man has worked out his own standards of right and wrong, justice and injustice, and striven to live by them. Of course as Christians we are different. Yes, but in what way are we different? Since we were converted a new sense of righteousness has been developed in us, with the result that we, too, are, quite rightly, occupied with the question of good and evil. But have we realized that for us the starting point is a different one? Christ is for us the Tree of Life. We do not begin from the matter of ethical right and wrong. We do not start from that other tree. We begin from *him;* and the whole question for us is one of life.

Nothing has done greater damage to our Christian testimony than our trying to be right and demanding right of others. We become preoccupied with what is and what is not right. We ask ourselves, *Have we been justly or unjustly treated?* and we think thus to vindicate our actions. But that is not our standard. The whole question for us is one of cross-bearing. You ask me, "Is it right for someone to strike my cheek?" I reply, "Of course not! But the question is, do you only want to be right?" As Christians our standard of living can never be "right or wrong" but the Cross. The principle of the Cross is our principle of conduct. Praise God that he makes his sun to shine on the evil and the good. With him it is a question of his grace and not of right or wrong. But that is to be our standard also: "Forgiving each other, even as God also in Christ forgave you" (4:32). "Right or wrong" is the principle of the Gentiles and tax gatherers. My life is to be governed by the principle of the Cross and the perfection of the Father: "Ye therefore shall be perfect, as your heavenly Father is perfect." - *Watchman Nee (Sit, Walk, Stand)*

Wicked Christianity

I

Thou believest that there is one God; thou doest well: the devils also believe, and tremble. (James 2:19)

Modern Christianity is fractured. In its current condition, the title of "Christian" represents a wide spectrum of beliefs and practices. This includes the ultra-moralistic conservatives, highly intellectual/philosophers, and experiential seekers. Unfortunately, doctrines held at different points along the spectrum of theologies tend to contradict other doctrines. In fact, when two Christians from different perspectives get together, there is a greater chance for disagreement than agreement.

This contradiction has not been missed by the lost. There have been several statistical demonstrations recently showing the rise of conversions to Islam, Mormonism, and Agnosticism. According to a study by the Pew Research Center, 44% of Americans belong to a faith different from the one in which they were raised. Christianity has increasingly become a source of mockery and disdain within America and other countries, not because of the message of the Gospel, but rather, because of the hypocrisy displayed in the lives of those who call themselves Christians.

Christianity, in its current state, is broken and in need of repair. This is a broad claim and requires explanation. It needs to be understood, that it is Christianity that needs to change, not the Gospel. The Gospel is not broken and it does not need to be fixed. The Gospel is the only hope for each and every one of us. Without it, none of us would have any hope of surviving the coming judgment. It is both true and infallible. It is not the Gospel that needs to be changed, but the church that needs to repent. We, as Christians, need to remember and proclaim the entire Gospel, not simply the version that is deemed acceptable in this modern, self-driven society.

The Word shows us that our adversary knows God's Word. In fact, he knows it much better than most Christians. While Satan hates all of God's Word, he knows that attacking the Word directly will only drive more people to it. He has taken a much more subtle tactic, and it has earned him the title: the Father of Lies. Instead of contradicting the Word, he highlights one section so that it overshadows the rest. He highlights God's love and downplays His wrath. Even more so, the adversary highlights God's grace and distracts us from His Holiness. In the most damaging blow, he shouts that it is not our place to judge one another, while hiding the fact that God will judge all men. History has shown us that, eventually, people will forget that there is more to the story and all we are left with is a wicked Christianity.

In its current state, Christianity is comprised of a generation of Christians that have never heard the whole Gospel. As a result, those who think they are learning about the Gospel are actually being taught a compromised message of spiritual growth. The enemy is proud that so many have been trapped by his subtle deception. This trap centers on two ideas, the first is that sin is all about behavior and the second is that the solution to the problem of sin is a better understanding of the Gospel. These beliefs are the root that feeds the fruit of hypocrisy in the church.

The message of the Gospel is that Jesus came and shed His blood so that those who are born of the flesh might, through belief, escape condemnation and have eternal life (John 3:1-21). It is very Biblical that there are sinful behaviors; however, the abundance of sinful behaviors in a person's life are the fruit of a person's heart before the Lord.

"And this is the condemnation, that light is come into the world, and men loved darkness rather than the light, because their deeds were evil" John 3:19.

Here, Jesus highlights the basic attribute of our fallen nature: we do not believe that anyone (including God) has the right to judge us; therefore, we run from all light. The Word never describes each individual behavior as the problem. Each individual behavior provides a glimpse into the heart of the person responsible for them. Each sin that the sinner commits is a living example that the Holy Spirit can use to show a man his true nature and standing before God. In other words, each sin is proof of our desperate need for salvation and an open sore for conviction to grasp. By turning the focus away from our position before God and onto every behavior, Satan has been able to produce a society where being a Christian simply means to be a person living a moral life. There is no longer a need for conversion in this message. For this reason, morality becomes a roadblock to the Gospel, instead of being evidence of it.

Once a person has come to the realization that he rightly deserves judgment, the second of the two traps comes into play. This is the trap of a false solution. Satan has, both subtly and effectively, changed the teaching of "repent and believe the Gospel" (Mark 1:15) to "understand the Gospel and integrate it into your daily life". Jesus taught about the specific need to be born of the spirit (John 3:5). By providing us with the Gospel, He has not given us the means to live better lives. He made the offer to change our nature (rebirth us into the spirit). The blood sacrifice was needed to satisfy the penalty for our sin. However, that only puts us in the position to believe on the Son.

"For every one that doeth evil hateth the light, neither cometh to the light, lest his deeds should be reproved. But he that doeth truth cometh to the light, that his deeds may be made manifest, that they are wrought in God" John 3:20-21

Jesus makes it clear in this passage that belief is necessary for the new birth. The proof of this regeneration is that the new person will seek to be judged by God. Jesus speaks of a belief that is, both, an active rejection of one's own judgement and an adoption of God's judgement. The fundamental effect of the Gospel is to highlight an individual's personal, underlying belief that God is a bad guy that refuses to acknowledge our goodness. This belief is so fundamental to our fallen condition that it must be revealed by the Holy Spirit through conviction. This is the reason that specific behaviors are discussed in the Word. Behaviors, and how we respond to them, are outward manifestations (fruit) of the nature of a man.

There is a lie that is fundamental to our fallen state. It is a lie that *preceded* all sin! Without this lie being believed, the Fall could have never occurred. The lie is that God is a mean God who is keeping good things away from us, and that His goal is to limit our own personal and spiritual growth. This lie took root in the heart of man *before* he fell to sin. (James 1:14-15) Remember the lie that the serpent used in the garden? This lie had to take root before any outward behavior of sin could possibly manifest itself.

Genesis 3:4-5: "And the serpent said unto the woman, Ye shall not surely die: **For God doth know that in the day ye eat thereof, then your eyes shall be opened, and ye shall be as gods, knowing good and evil."**

Now, we know the serpent was lying then he said, "Ye shall not surely die." God said they would die and that was most surely true. However, at first reading, it sounds as though the serpent was lying when he said, "...ye shall be as gods, knowing good and evil." This is not he case. Genesis 3:22 goes on to say, *"And the Lord God said, Behold, the man is become as one of us, to know good and evil."* This shows that the serpent's deception was much more subtle. While he evidently gave correct information, in doing so, he presented God as someone who was keeping Adam and Eve from something good. This is the root of lust. He was presenting Eve with the opportunity to judge God with her own judgment. Eve judged the situation for herself and believed a conclusion that did not originate from God. It is this act of unbelief that brought forth the fruit of sin, and with it, the fall.

As a result of believing this lie, and subsequently sinning before God, we each have this fundamental ability to tell the difference between good and evil (Genesis 3:22). As a part of our fallen condition, each man carries with him the belief that (since we are able to judge between good and evil) our judgment on the matter bears just as much weight as God's judgment (for we have become as gods, according to our deception). We also believe that our moral development is evidence of a spiritual evolution that will end in the completion of our "godhood". This provides an underlying belief that God is an enemy to our own growth and development and that submission and belief in Him is akin to giving up the rights to our own destiny. It is this belief that is at the root of all of our rebellion. Part of the problem is that this rebellion is so fundamental to our daily life that we do not believe it exists. It is simply who we are. It is the complete rejection of this rebellion (repentance) that Jesus is requiring in John 3.

****

The practical effect of this foundational belief is easy to identify. It only requires a simple social experiment to see this belief in action. Go to the mall, park, or any other place where you will find people with whom you can start a conversation. After your initial greetings, ask them if they believe that insulting someone out of anger is bad enough to warrant hell. When they answer "no", which 99% of people will, read Matt 5:22, 1 John 3:15, and Revelations 21:8. These three verses clearly describe a murderous heart and it's eternal reward. However, it will quickly be evident that their belief is based on more than just the Bible, and that what is written in the Bible is not considered enough to change their mind.

The vast majority of the people that you interact with in this experiment will respond by using the phrase "Well, I believe..." or "Well, I think..." or even "I understand that's what the Bible says, but I...". Even if the individual actually agrees with the point of view described in the Biblical reference, the reason that the person will give for the topic's *goodness* or *badness* will be based in what they think / believe, rather than in the Biblical reasons given. In other words, their judgment is not based on the Bible, but rather, how they perceive good and evil. If the Bible is correct, it is merely a coincidence that the Bible agrees with their point of view. When someone takes this stand, the Bible may act as a point of reference, but they are not setting it as the absolute authority on the topic (even ahead of their own opinions).

Due to the post modern environment that has defined our society for the past thirty years, when someone responds by stating their own belief, they are really saying that both what they believe and what the Bible says are equally valid. It is this response that the Church is designed to overcome. This response is, in essence, "spiritual self-defense." Man's dead nature actively fights the conviction that would bring it to life. If they were to truly lay down their own judgments on the matter, the only course of action remaining would be to compare their own life to the Word.

It is during this act of comparison that the God that loves the world draws an individual to salvation through the conviction of sin.

The fallen man reacts defensively to this spiritual interaction because it can only end in its death. At our core, we truly believe that we are inherently good and that, while we make mistakes, we are growing into the best person that we can be. We may believe that we need some help from God along the way, but the idea that we are inherently wicked and need our nature changed is seen as an insult to our spirituality. It is this main belief that needs to die on the altar of repentance. This is something that nobody wants to hear.

2

The ideas of good and evil are literally as old as creation itself. The first time the word "good" appears in the Bible is Genesis 1:4. The only concept that can be described as more fundamental is that of light and darkness. In fact, it was the creation of light that God first identified as being good.

It is in Genesis 2:9 that describes the way we first came into contact with the idea of good and evil. It was the tree of the knowledge of good and evil. Until then, all that Adam and Eve knew was what God told them directly. What a way to live! Now, if you will remember from Genesis 2:16-17, the effects of this tree were never meant to be felt by mankind. Adam was never supposed to have the knowledge of good and evil, yet it was this knowledge that the serpent claimed would make them as gods (Genesis 3:5). Satan claimed that God was keeping that knowledge for Himself in order to keep them under control.

Now, we know the end of the story of Eden in the Bible. Eve was deceived by the serpent, and Adam disobeyed God by choosing the deception over the Word of God. It was through this act of disobedience, the eating of the tree of the knowledge of good and evil, that the ability to tell the difference between good and evil was passed down to us. However, according to the original design, we were meant to depend on God for this information. It was designed to be a dynamic source of intimacy between ourselves and the Father.

That is the key point which renders spiritually vulgar our modern use of the word "good." Whether something is good, or

13

evil, is not nearly as important as who is declaring it to be so. We have believed the lie that, since we can now tell that there is a difference between good and evil, then our judgments bear the same eternal significance as God's judgment on right and wrong.

Let's go back to the social test. Go out into public and ask people if they believe that premarital sex is evil. When they say, "no," read I Corinthians 6:9-10 with them. Through this passage, it will become apparent that their judgment and God's judgment are different. Whose judgment is greater, theirs or God's? Since God is the only one who has the ultimate ability to judge something to be either good or evil, any instance in which we do so ourselves (as opposed to referring to His judgment) is simply an act of self-proclaimed righteousness. It is through this that we learn who is actively being proclaimed as ruler of one's life: God or self.

This belief defines our fallen state: that the knowledge of good and evil is something that we can attain and perfect in our own spiritual evolution. We hold to the illusion that our values and judgments bear eternal weight. If we believe that we can be as gods, then we also believe that is how God achieved His Godhood. We demonstrate that we do not believe our own sin is a problem because we operate on the premise that, even though we aren't perfect, we are constantly learning and growing. We believe that, because we are learning from our mistakes, we are growing into the person that we were meant to be. This is why we interpret God's conviction as his tool for holding us back from our own spiritual growth. If instead, we truly believed that we could not be good apart from Him, we would stop trying to strengthen our own spirituality and cry out to Him for what He says we need.

Fallen man cannot permit himself to simply cling to His Word and judgments. Like the teenager that believes he shouldn't have to listen to his parents because he knows how to make decisions, we want to stand on our own two feet. We demand the right to make our own judgments and walk in our own counsel. Try telling someone that something they are doing is wrong, and then back it up Biblically. Unless the person is born again and walking with the Lord, the first reaction will be "Who are you to judge me? I'm a Christian, too." This is usually stated as if this statement of being a Christian changes the fact that they are walking against its tenets at the moment. The idea that they are displaying fruit that hints at their eternal destination is not a problem to them.

One social evidence of this foundational belief is found throughout entertainment and the arts. How many of our stories revolve around the hero's journey? The hero's journey is a story in which the protagonist is faced with obstacles that force him to face his own weakness. These challenges require him to strenthen his will and resolve in order to grow into the conquering hero the plot requires. This theme is so predominant throughout history because we can relate to the hero's persona and growth as if it were our own.

The demand to judge things for ourselves was the root that allowed all sin to grow in the heart of man. However, it is not sufficient to simply alter that demand. On the contrary, once we separated our own judgements from God's, we separated ourselves from Him completely. Once this demand was made, sinful behavior was the only possible outcome. This created a gulf that we had no hope of bridging. While most look at life as a journey to better ourselves and to grow, life itself is nothing more than a period of probation. It is not a probationary period for us to overcome our own sin, but rather, a delay of judgment that provides an individual has the opportunity to be regenerated through the Blood before final judgement must take place.

Once Adam and Eve sinned, man became spiritually dead, they (and each of us as their children) required being "born in the spirit" to escape the final consequence of our dead nature. Even as God cursed the ground, He set everything in motion so that this issue of sin could be taken care of. However, as a result of the fall, man gained an ability that he was never supposed to have: the knowledge of good and evil.

It is this ability that has deceived men into believing that he is not spiritually dead, but rather, alive and simply in need of guidance. Satan uses this ability to teach the idea that this life is about man overcoming his sin nature and integrating the lessons of Christ into his life so that man can once again be allowed into heaven. This deception emphasizes the idea of the Christian walk as a "path" and the importance of having a set of "beliefs". This is the essential tactic by which Satan has been able to twist and change the Gospel in the modern church.

3

There is a wickedness is modern Christianity that has been slowly working its way into pulpits all across the nation for the past 40 years. It has become so pervasive, that it seems to be fundamental to modern Christianity. At it's core, this wickedness can be attributed to rejecting the Biblical truth that, "...there is none that seeketh after God." (Romans 3:11) We have forgotten that man's heart is fundamentally set in opposition to the heart of the Father. We have not only forgotten this fact, but we have embraced a Gospel that provides a way for each rich young ruler to become a good Christian without having his fundamental sin nature dealt with at the Cross.

While there are many that seek a god that matches their understanding of what God should be like, Romans makes it clear that none seek God as He actually is: the one whose knowledge and judgments trump our own. The wickedness of the modern church began when it started to merge its two main purposes: preaching the Gospel to the lost and preparing and equipping the saints. When the church forgets that there is a fundamental difference between those who are born of flesh and those who are born of spirit, it simply begins to teach all men how to be Christians.

While the Gospel is truly the Good News, it is only good news to those that respond with humility and repentance. For those that refuse to humble themselves and repent before a Holy God, it is the damning evidence that makes their decent into hell completely just. It is this second aspect of the Gospel that the modern church has sidestepped. The difficult part of the Gospel is no longer preached because it is deemed too offensive. However, when we sidestep the offensive nature of the Cross, we open the door for a "humility free" salvation. By removing the presence of death, hell, and the grave from the Gospel message, the modern church has subtly changed the message from "come and Christ will set you free" to "come and experience your freedom in Christ". The difference between these two messages is not merely semantic. It is all encompassing. It deals with the posture in which men come before God: as good men in need of spiritual enlightenment or as dead men in bondage to their own sin.

Teaching someone how to be a Christian can only occur with an assumption of salvation. This assumption is made evident when the topics of sin and repentance are glossed over, eliminating the experience of conviction. Once salvation is assumed, ministry is then reduced to understanding Christian values, behavior modification, and reducing the frequency and consequence of sin. This is equivalent to teaching someone how to be born, or how to become alive.

This is wickedness for two reasons. First, teaching someone how to do something (how to become a Christian) also teaches them that they have the ability to do the thing being taught. The Bible makes it clear that there is nothing that man can do to earn salvation. There is no set of morals that can be followed or doctrine that can be adhered to that will open the doors of heaven.

Second, the act of teaching someone to be a Christian is wicked because it ignores man's need for conversion. This means that they are taking God's role out of the equation. Romans makes it quite clear that the measure of faith that is required for a fallen man to respond to a person's individual offer of salvation is, in itself, a gift from the Lord. In other words, God draws a man to salvation, convicts, provides the faith needed to repent and believe. He then, sovereignly, gives the individual the opportunity to respond to what the Lord has revealed about their nature (by the means that the Lord has provided).

When an individual responds to the Holy Ghost during this process with repentance, there is a fundamental change within the nature of the person. The "spirit-man" is made alive and now has the ability to grow in the knowledge and stature of the Lord, just like a child can grow to be like his parents. Rather than showing people their need for regeneration, the Church is teaching them to be Christians. They teach that each one can be a good Christian person, simply by understanding, acknowledging, and emotionally eperiencing the Bible.

Now, teaching is a very important role of the church. However, this role is limited to teaching someone how to grow as something they already are, not how to *become* something that they aren't. There is a major difference between teaching someone how to walk out their faith (and strengthen the new creature that God has made them to be) and teaching someone how to become a Christian. By doing this, the church is only able to create numerous "nominal" and "carnal" Christians who have never actually come to a saving knowledge of, through personal interaction with, the Father.

If someone is born again, the Biblical teachings of living sinlessly, growing in Holiness, and developing character traits (charity, meekness, humility, etc), while being difficult to receive by the flesh, will be a source of life to the living, Godly spirit-man that was created during salvation. If someone has been taught to be a Christian, they don't have this living, Godly spirit-man living within them, so there is no life in them to grow through the teachings of the Word. So, if there is nothing in them to grow, there is only the flesh to keep under control and satisfy.

This is the source of many crisis of faith. When men know what to believe, but have not been made new and capable of walking out this belief, they are stuck as a dead man looking at life. They have no way to touch or experience it. However, they know that, if what they believed was true, then they should be able to experience it completely. So, since they say they believe, why can't they experience it? Sadly, instead of running away from this catch-22 and toward the Cross, men try to solve their crisis by looking for a preacher who phrases their teachings in a way to satisfy their current crisis. This latter example is, unfortunately, where the majority of the modern church spends its time.

****

The heart [is] deceitful above all [things], and desperately wicked: who can know it? (Jeremiah 17:9)

This trap that has been set for the church through a focus on behavior has distorted the Gospel message and distracted the church from what the lost desperately need to hear. One fruit of this distraction is the idea of morality.

It is true that, as a result of conversion, an individual will actively behave in a manner that pleases his Savior. The types of behavior that proceed from the daily life of such a convert will appear to the world as very moral. However, morality is not the standard that a regenerated man seeks to meet. He strives for holiness, driven by the conviction of the Holy Spirit. This personal interaction between God and man is the source of goodness that can please God. All other reasons for good behavior build self-righteousness.

It has never been the role of the church to eradicate sinful behaviors. Through preaching (and requiring) morality, the church has simply provided the lost with proverbial fig leaves. By doing so, however, the church has denied the lost with the flesh-humbling, and spirit-convicting, truth that both the sinful behavior they just committed, and their internal desire to continue in sinful behaviors, is evidence of their condition before a Holy God. As a result, the majority of society has a strong connection between "living right" and being a "good Christian" and no connection between their motivations, behaviors, and their state before the Almighty God.

In modern society, morality plays a large part in Christianity. If you were to talk to someone on the street and ask them if they thought that they were a good person, most people would answer by saying, "Yes." If you were to follow up that question by asking what makes them a good person, their answer would most likely fall into one of two categories: behavior or values. For instance, one popular answer is that they have done more good things than bad. What is more important (and damning), however, is that they believe the good things that they have done are more in line with who they are. Since this what they believe, they think that their good works will have a stronger sway when it comes to their ultimate judgment.

Good values can also be attributed to a person believing that they are good. This type of person knows many spiritual things. They know the teachings of the Bible, and possibly other sources. They have a strong personal association with these values, and feel as though, because they know how to tell the difference between right and wrong, and can back up their knowledge from "good books," then they are good.

Even though these two ideas (good behavior and good values) are in complete contradiction to the Great Commission, they are the cornerstones of the modern Christian message being preached throughout America. This has allowed an atmosphere of *perceived* Christianity. It is a Christianity that encourages someone to lead a better life with fewer consequences of sins while leaving their eternal condition in peril. It is this culture of acknowledging Biblical truths (knowing right) and emphasizing morality (living right) that falsely provides each individual with the assurance of their own goodness and assurance of heaven.

The wickedness of this preaching will be shown for what it is when each individual has their moment before the judgment Throne. Despite someone's morality and acknowledgement of the

Bible, unless someone has responded, with repentance, when the Holy Spirit convicts them of their condition before the Holy God, then they will hear what Jesus says in Matthew 7.

Many will say to me in that day, Lord, Lord, have we not prophesied in thy name? and in thy name have cast out devils? and in thy name done many wonderful works? And then will I profess unto them, I never knew you: depart from me, ye that work iniquity. (Matthew 7:22-23)

While, on its surface, morality seems like a set of Godly standards, it only keeps the lost individual from being able to hear the conviction of the Lord. Godly behavior is the fruit of the new motivation found within the heart of a convert. This motivation is obedience to God's Word. It is not the behavior alone that is godly, but rather the motivation that is godly because it is the result of a desire to please the Father. The goodness of the behavior is a secondary benefit that is used to demonstrate to the lost the goodness of the Savior. We are simply stewards of the grace that has been so freely given to us.

By equating godliness with behavior we open the door for counterfeit fruit to be accepted as genuine. We must encourage the examination of an individual's motivation. Behavior alone can be a false indicator of a person's standing before the Lord. It is possible to do something moral for ungodly reasons (look at the rich young ruler). However, a person's motivation before the Lord always speaks to the heart of the issue, or perhaps more poignantly, to the issue of the heart.

As a result of the fall, the strongest aspect of our fallen nature that keeps us from freely desiring humble repentance is our ability to distinguish between good and evil. Our fight with God can be boiled down to the fact that we do not agree with God's judgment of our nature as wicked. We fundamentally disagree that we are fully deserving of hell. We resent the fact that we are going to hell because it is not our own judgments that will send us there. We believe that we are going to hell because of God, rather than because of our sinful nature. How wicked indeed! As a result, rather than being good news, the Gospel is seen as a slap in the face to the lost man.

For the preaching of the Cross is to them that perish foolishness; but unto us which are saved it is the power of God. (1 Corinthians 1:18)

The modern church has, in the name of evangelism, sidestepped this issue by preaching the Gospel with a spin. Instead of requiring the lost man to confront his enmity with God, they provide a Gospel that tells them the consequences for their sin has been taken away and that all they need to do is acknowledge God's Word as true and try to follow Biblical principles. This allows the lost man to have a stamp of Christian approval while continuing on his life's journey of growth and spiritual development.

Morality is the natural outflow of this compromised Gospel. By providing people with a standard to live up to, the church is feeding, rather than fighting, the most foundational and wicked aspect of our fallen nature. By switching the main focus from the motivation of the heart to behavior, the church is teaching people how to strengthen their ability to tell the difference between good and evil. Remember, our ability to tell the difference between good and evil is the fundamental reason we hold for not needing the Gospel. This ability automatically makes anyone an enemy who does not agree with our views, including God. The stronger we hold on to our morality and our good values, the less we believe that we need God.

This highlights the devilish nature of Satan's distraction. By diverting the focus from our personal motivation and nature before a Holy God to a need for good values and behavior, the church is teaching people how to sing God's praises while traveling the wide road to hell. The good values that the church is teaching are Biblical ideals, but since they are out of Biblical order, the vast majority of Christians believe they have something that they do not. For example, they may know the Biblical truth that lying is ungodly, however, instead of being confronted with the fact that their lies are evidence that they are liars and that Revelations 21:8 applies to them, the compromised Gospel teaches them to stop lying and learn the value of the truth. The stronger that a person becomes in *his own* judgment of the value of truth, the less he will be concerned with *God's* judgment concerning his nature before Him. Not only are people becoming decreasingly concerned with God's judgments concerning their life, their Christianity is allowing them to become more self-assured of their own goodness.

The fear of the Lord [is] the instruction of wisdom; and before honour [is] humility. (Proverbs 15:33)

Wicked Christianity

4

Your glorying [is] not good. Know ye not that a little leaven leaveneth the whole lump? (I Corinthians 5:6)

Within today's Christianity, we are overlooking the truth that there are two different types of people: those born of the flesh (lost/unregenerate) and those born of the spirit (saved/ regenerated). Instead of preaching, and looking for evidence of, conversion, the modern church is treating everyone as if they are simply in different places in their Christian walk. By doing this, the modern church is accepting as regenerate, those that have no real conversion in their life. This removes any possibility of hope for a sinner, because the one thing that the lost person needs, is the one thing that the church is no longer preaching.

Today's church produces two different types of Christians. The first type of Christian is exemplified by Paul and the woman at the well. Both had a life changing moment wherein Jesus showed them their fallen nature and offered His eternal life. Let's use the woman at the well as an example. The woman, and the corresponding type of Christian, did not respond by integrating Jesus' view on morality so that she could then lead a more pure life. She did not become motivated to change her lifestyle so that adultery was no longer a part of it. She recognized Jesus for who He was and brought everyone within hearing distance to see how Jesus could change their life as well.

It is this type of conversion that results in a fundamental shift in a person's understanding concerning their nature. It is a deep change from having "right beliefs" to being changed by God from the inside. This type of Christian is fully convinced of two things: the greatness of God and their sinful state. This Christian walk begins when the person is under the preaching of the Word of God. During the preaching, the Lord begins to draw that person to Himself. The Lord does this by highlighting the person's sin-based need of a Savior. Then, if they are willing to repent and believe in the Gospel, He will give Salvation without restraint.

Once this act of salvation is complete, it is the rudder by which the rest of their life is steered. This type of Christian passionately reads and obeys the Bible because he knows it gets him closer to the Savior whom they personally know. They obey out of love, not requirement; and, while they do personally mature in their faith, that maturity is a byproduct, not a goal.

The second type of Christian walk is simply a result of an understanding of the Bible. This person is trying to become a better person by learning all the good teachings of God and trying to integrate them into their life. This type of Christian recognizes that God is Good and that His ways need to be learned and His laws need to be obeyed. They believe that to be a good person, they must be a good Christian. They also know that being a good Christian pays off with good things happening in their life. These two things (learning and obeying) describe the nature of this walk. However, they are not done out of a sense of belonging to a Savior, they are carried out because of they are the tools that are available for their own personal and spiritual growth. It is the Christianity of self-improvement through understanding God.

This type of Christian, much like the rich young ruler of Luke 18, rather than being in need of conversion, considers himself able to understand, and integrate godly principles into his life. He knows the truth that he has been taught and he has centered his life around it. This person is fully confident of their spiritual ability to stand on his own two feet and walk with God. His only real need of Jesus is to use Him as a source of information and as a model deity to mimic. Even after a face to face interaction with God, he is only left with the sad realization that his fundamental beliefs push him to prefer an eternity in hell to genuine belief.

Wicked Christianity

5

In John 4, Jesus began traveling from Judea to Galilee; however, in His love for His creation, he needed to stop in Samaria to have an interaction with people that needed to Him.   He stopped at Jacob's well and, while His disciples went to the nearest city, found a Samaritan woman coming to the well to draw water. She was a woman who was living a normal human life, taking care of the major needs of her life: safety, security, and satisfaction. She would be described, in present day, as someone who's doing her best in the middle of difficult situations. She sees herself as a good person that has gone through difficult things in her life.

Jesus began to interact with her in a way that disrupted the natural flow of her life.   He asked her to get Him some water. Instead of responding to His request, the woman reacts to His breach of the cultural norms.   She says little more than "why are you talking to me?" By doing this, she is attempting to push Him away.   As a Jew, Jesus' interaction is more intimate than she would like it to be.   However, despite her initial reaction, Jesus' goal is to get much more personal.

Jesus begins illuminate the type of relief she could obtain through Him.   He says, *"If thou knewest the gift of God, and who it is that saith to thee, Give me to drink; thou wouldest have asked of him, and he would have given thee living water."   (John 4:10)* When she continues to doubt, He continues, *"Whosoever drinketh of this water shall thirst again: But whosoever drinketh of the water that I shall give him shall never thirst; but the water that I shall give him shall be in him a well of water springing up into everlasting life." (John 4:13-14)*

So far, Jesus has been expressing two different ideas: her need and His ability to completely satisfy her need. As He continued talking about her thirst and His ability to completely satisfy it, she began to realize that He was offering something that, if it were real, would have been immeasurably valuable to her. So she asks Him to give it to her. However, Jesus knew that wanting fulfillment of her needs and needing the fulfiller are two completely different things. At this point, the water He mentioned was more important to her than Jesus was.

In response to her request for the water, Jesus told her to call on her husband. He knew, of course, that she had been married five times, and that she was now living with a sixth man. Now He was getting very personal. By asking about her husband, he put a spotlight on the area in her life that had the deepest sin: adultery. It was her deepest sin because, even though it was obviously condemned in the scriptures, she believed it had been justifiable due to her circumstances. She was able to reason away the fact that it was sin, and thereby, no longer consider herself a sinner. Instead, she thought of herself as someone doing what she needed to get along in her life.

At this command, the woman responded with a guarded truth. She admitted that she was not married, but was unwilling to admit her personal sin in this area. Out of His goodness, Jesus did this for her. He pointed out the truth concerning her adultery.

This very act, by any other person, would have been a condemnation. Even from Jesus, it surely would have been a condemnation, had she not responded with such belief and affection. Here is the key element of the Gospel that must be grasped: the answer can only be offered after the Lord has identified, in the most personal way, the person's sin.

It needs to be highlighted how strong our reaction of spiritual self-defense can be. Every time that Jesus tries to get personal with this woman, she moves the conversation to a social topic (in response to His first request) or vague spiritual idea (in response to her sin). We must not acquiesce and accept a general statement of understanding from the lost man as personal repentance and belief.

As the story continues, Jesus turns her spiritual conversation concerning *a* Messiah into a specific conversation that she was talking to *the* Messiah. When faced with the confrontation of her nature before the God that was standing in front of her, she ran and began to tell the entire town who was in their midst and what He was there to do. As a result, Jesus was besought to stay.

When He tarried, many believed. Their faith began by hearing her testimony: *"Come, see a man, which told me all things that ever I did: is this not the Christ?"* (John 4:29). It ended with everyone else seeing for themselves that Jesus was *their* Messiah.

John 4:29 shows that she had a very personal understanding of what Paul said in I Timothy 1:15, "This is a faithful saying, and worthy of all acceptation, that Christ came in to the world to save sinners, of whom I am chief."

Wicked Christianity

6

And a certain ruler asked him, saying, Good Master, what shall I do to inherit eternal life? And Jesus said unto him, Why callest thou me good? none is good, save one, that is, God. Thou knowest the commandments, Do not commit adultery, Do not kill, Do not steal, Do not bear false witness, Honour thy father and thy mother. And he said, All these have I kept from my youth up. Now when Jesus heard these things, he said unto him, Yet lackest thou one thing: sell all that thou hast, and distribute unto the poor, and thou shalt have treasure in heaven: and come, follow me. And when he heard this, he was very sorrowful: for he was very rich. And when Jesus saw that he was very sorrowful, he said, How hardly shall they that have riches enter into the kingdom of God! For it is easier for a camel to go through a needle's eye, than for a rich man to enter into the kingdom of God. And they that heard it said, Who then can be saved? And he said, The things which are impossible with men are possible with God. (Luke 18:18-27)

As we have just read, this certain ruler came to Jesus seeking the path to eternal life. He had been to (the equivalent of) church all his life. He had done everything that that church has told him is godly. By his own admission, he had lived a moral life, honored the Sabbath, and kept the commandments by making the appropriate sacrifices for sin that the Old Testament law required. The only problem the ruler had is that he was sadly ignorant of why Jesus came to earth in the first place.

Jesus had come to seek and save the lost (Luke 19:10, 1 Tim. 1:15). Instead of seeing himself as needing the Messiah, this ruler saw himself as capable of following the law. Through his first question, *"Good Master, what shall I do to inherit eternal life?"* it is evident that he believed himself to be capable of following whatever new principle that he expected to hear from Jesus. He did not see himself as lost and in need of a Savior, just in need of a teacher.

This young ruler was standing in the presence of God Himself, and all he wanted to know was about the next step in his spiritual walk. Jesus, Himself, was not the object of this young ruler's search. He was simply the source of the information the young ruler believed was needed to inherit eternal life. He would have been the model "Christ follower," if he had lived today. He was never born again (even though Jesus preached its necessity) but he used all of his human ability to be a good person, learn, and give credence to what he knew of God.

Unlike what Paul said in I Timothy 1:15, the rich young ruler, and modern day Christ-follower, would have said that the Gospel is summed up in this: "Since Christ died, we can now reach within us, recognize our spirituality and use our nature to become more like our Creator."

Jesus pointed to the one thing that this young ruler lacked: a humble need for a Savior. Had he believed this, then all the riches that he possessed could not have stood in his way. Zacchaeus provides the perfect testimony of this truth. Rather than having too much wealth to give away, the rich young ruler viewed his wealth as proof of his inherent value. So, what he heard Jesus say was not simply "Give away all you have" but also "Let go of every self-righteous belief you hold." He was simply not willing to do this. As a result, what could have turned into an offer of salvation turned into a condemnation. The very chains that Jesus highlighted to break became the chains that dragged his soul into eternal flames.

Unlike the interaction with the woman at the well, when Jesus pinpointed this man's core sin, the ruler did not get excited that his foundational sin had been uncovered (and could, subsequently, be taken care of by Jesus). Instead, he went away sorrowful because the thing that Jesus identified to be sin was the one thing that he valued in himself.

****

After years of transition within the modern church, we have lost the awareness of the need for conversion and regeneration for one to become a believer. We have become so focused on growing the "church" that we have traded the fruit of salvation for a simple prayer and statement of belief. As long as we elicit one of these we readily accept the person as a believer. As a result, the modern church has become focused on educating and encouraging anyone who claims to be a Christian, as well as pressuring outward morality. In the process, the church has refused to be what it was designed to be. It fails to preach repentance and remission of sins (Luke 24:47) so that the Holy Spirit can convict of sin, righteousness and judgment (John 16:8). This has produced a church that values image and experience over holiness. As a result, while church growth is at an all time high, the morality within the church is, at best, equal with the world, and in reality, far worse.

All Christian growth must begin, and continue, from the specific interaction between the Holy Spirit and the individual. It is an unpopular statement, however it must be said, that anything other than interaction between a Holy God and a spiritually dead sinner (even if it results in the words "I believe in Jesus" being spoken) provides a *false conversion*.

In 2 Corinthians, we are told to examine ourselves to see if we are of the faith. It is of supreme importance for each believer to know whether they are relying on God's righteousness or their own. In order for someone to be "of the faith" they must have had a "Damascus Road" experience of their own. They must have had an experience where, through the foolishness of preaching, the Holy Spirit shows them their specific, personal state of sin before a Holy God and cry out in obedient repentance at His free offer of salvation.

This is not to say that there are extra steps, beyond belief, needed for salvation. John 3:16 makes it clear that, "whosoever believeth on Him" shalt be saved. Repentance *is* the first act of belief; to turn from one's own judgments to that of the Lord's. This simply describes the dynamic in which such a belief can take place and what will come out of it. Jesus said that, "No man can come to me, except the Father which hath sent me draw him" (John 6:44). This shows that this belief can only take place during a personal, and specific, interaction between the Father and the individual. The Lord continues to speak to this through Paul in Romans 10:14 and

I Corinthians 1:21, that hearing the Word preached is a vital part of the dynamic for someone to be able to believe.

However, once the Word is preached and the dead man's "spiritual self defense" has been laid aside, the real miracle begins. In the individual's perspective, the offer of salvation changes from: "God died to save the world from perishing" to "I deserve to perish, but Jesus died so that I might live." The individual then has the option to respond to the Lord's offer in faith, or reject it. This is the crux of the issue. To respond in faith (to believe) requires the rejection of our dead man, his desires and judgments. This is called repentance. The individual can respond like Saul (Paul) by rejecting his former life, or like the rich young ruler by continuing to embrace it. (Acts 3:19-23)

During conviction, an individual is being given the ability to repent. The Lord responds to their belief by regenerating their dead hearts into a new creature. This is a specific, and highly personal, act that occurs in one event. Paul calls it *conversion* in the Acts. This new creature has a passionate affection for their Savior that the dead man was incapable of experiencing (let alone acting on). Their motivation is not in the inherent rightness of the behavior, but to naturally please their Savior by what is written in His Word. By allowing us to respond in repentance, the Holy Spirit teaches the new man his primary function in this world: to actively shed the remnants of this world (in behaviors *and* affections) and press on towards Holiness. The believer cares not for morals, but rather, Holiness! This passionate fruits of repentance do not make a person a Christian, instead they are the natural product of someone that has been made into a Christian.

As it stands, the modern church is filled, and in some cases *led*, by people who claim to be Christian, yet they are still unregenerate and spiritually dead. It is time for the complete message of Jesus to be preached in this world. The Gospel is not simply a concept meant to inspire people to believe. Pastors: do not bow to the world's demands to eliminate judgment from what you preach. That is what the majority have done over the past thirty years. We are called to preach what God says they need to hear, not simply what they are willing to hear. When the church started requiring the adherence to biblical tenants instead of preaching conversion, it began to reinforce man's fallen nature. The result of that compromise is that we have a fractured and wicked Christianity.

Wise but Unjust

Wicked Christianity

I

Be not wise in thine own eyes: Fear the Lord and depart from evil. (Proverbs 3:7)

Satan's deception in the garden was a masterful bait and switch. When we thought that we were gaining the ability to be more like God, we really gained the ability to see ourselves as god. Unfortunately, this removed our ability to see God as the source of good. We believe that we have joined Him in that role. We gave up far more than we gained.

The result of the fall is two fold. First, our view of God changed. In our eyes, God changed from being the source of goodness and truth to the manipulator that was demanding that we see things His way. By adding the ability to distinguish between good and evil, we replaced God as our source for knowledge. With our ability to judge things for ourselves, we became self-sufficient in our own minds.

This dynamic is inherently damning. Since God is the originator of all truth and goodness, no matter how closely our judgments come to resembling His, we are still their source. We are not God, so in spite of our ability to judge good and evil, we can only produce self-serving darkness. However, since our darkness is made up of what we judge to be good, we are constantly at enmity with the One who dares condemn that which we esteem. This is why there can be no saving faith apart from repentance.

Fundamentally, we believe that, since we can distinguish between good and evil, our judgments should be respected as equally valid. This is the source of the second result of the fall. Our ability to know good and evil gives us a sense of control over our life. We do not simply stop at making judgments concerning good and evil, we actively operate based off of our own judgments. By doing so, we rule our lives by the things we decide are valuable. We view God as a threat because operating from His judgments requires us to be dethroned. Instead of having our identity as stewards of God's goodness, we operate as kings over our own kingdoms.

This is the dynamic that Jesus is presenting through the parable of the wise but unjust steward in found in Luke 16, Jesus has just finished giving the parable of the Prodigal Son and begins to tell another parable. It is about a master who has a steward that has been unfaithful: an unjust steward.

2

And he said also unto his disciples, There was a certain rich man, which had a steward; and the same was accused unto him that he had wasted his goods. And he called him, and said unto him, How is it that I hear this of thee? give an account of thy stewardship; for thou mayest be no longer steward. (Luke 16:1-2)

This is one of those passages of scripture where we find several verses that people tend to stick on their refrigerator. Verses like *"He that is faithful in that which is least is faithful also in much." (Luke 16:10)* These are sayings that have been trivialized in modern Christianity. It is very important, as familiar as some of these verses are, that they not be taken out of context. This passage could be very confusing. Therefore, we must examine it so that we can understand what the Lord is communicating through it.

We have an individual that has been unfaithful to his master and has been found out. Yet, after being found out, he continues in his unfaithfulness. Despite his unfaithfulness, his master calls him wise! These descriptions are seemingly contradictory.

While it is in verse 8 that he is deemed an unjust steward, this description it is fitting of him throughout. In the Greek, the word "unjust" means "full of iniquity and unrighteousness." According to this definition, the steward sees every situation through the lenses of iniquity. He is not merely doing something selfishly, or simply taking care of himself, he is full of iniquity. His primary method of operation is deceit.

In the beginning of the passage, it says that there was a certain rich man that had a steward. The steward was a man who has been put in charge of great wealth. It is important to note that, while he is in charge of the goods, they belong to the Master. He has demonstrated himself to be unjust in the way he wasted the goods.

The word "wasted" is key to understanding his unjust character. It does not mean that the steward lost all of his Master's money. When it is said that he "wasted" the Master's goods, it means that he used it in a way that misrepresented the Master. While they were in his charge, he used them in a way that was not intended. While he was operating out of what he judged to be good, he operated in a way that degraded the good name of his Master. As a result, he required that the steward give an account of his stewardship and he removed the steward from his position.

In this parable, as with all parables, Jesus is speaking on several levels. He is talking on the practical level, dealing with money and interacting with authority. However, He is also talking on a spiritual level. From this perspective, being removed from the position of the steward is comparable to dying. Jesus is telling us that our time here, the time that we have been living, is going to end and something else is going to come after it. The time we spend in our present condition (in the parable, the time of his stewardship) is very limited.

Then the steward said within himself, What shall I do? for my lord taketh away from me the stewardship (Luke 16:3)

Here, he has been told that he is not long for this world. He is told that he is going to have to give an account for everything that he has done during his time as a steward. His first question is "What shall I do?" He has just been told that he's going to die and that he's going to be held accountable. Had he been a just steward all along, he would have been asking this question well before now.

When he says, 'What shall I do," he means, "How can I take care of this?" It is in this inward question that he displays his heart of iniquity.

What shall I do? for my lord taketh away from me the stewardship

This shows the iniquity that is at the foundation of his unrighteousness. He is saying that it is the master's fault that he is losing his stewardship. Just as this steward, the unjust man sees is no connection between his unjust behavior and losing the stewardship (life). His death is not his fault or, at least, this is the way he views his current situation. He carries no blame for what is getting ready to occur in his life. Everything that he was required to give account for, was in his eyes, legitimate. This is the height of arrogance: saying in one's heart, "It's not my fault. The master is unfairly taking away from me all that I have."

There is an aspect to our condition that we don't lose when we're saved. While our sins have been wiped clean, we are stuck with our fallen nature until Glory. If iniquity could be summed up in one little idea, it would be our internal fight, or demand, to have our judgments acknowledged. It is the internal demand that says *I am right, I should to get what I want*, and that *I should be able to behave and be treated in the manner that I, not anyone else, get to choose.*

This inner demand, this iniquity, is in direct opposition to the way man was created. It prevents us from being able to care about something the way God does, and it renders us unable to love our Creator. It is this inner demand, this inner fight, that is at work within the heart of the steward as he states "My Lord hath taken from me the stewardship."

The reason that the steward is now losing the stewardship is simple. As a result of his iniquity, he was unable to value the character of the Master. All of his judgments worked towards building his own kingdom. Hence, he could do nothing but mar the Master's reputation. While he is about to have to give an account of his behavior, he sees himself in a position of self-defense, not legitimate judgment. His time is growing short and he is increasingly aware of his need to do something so that he might survive this transition.

How many people are living day to day that are, in their own little way, trying to cheat death? They are trying to console themselves with the belief that their actions will solve the problem of hell. This is the spiritual equivalent of the steward's next dilemma.

"I cannot dig; to beg I am ashamed." (Luke 16:3b)

Here, the steward is proclaiming his inability to provide for his own well being. This is his justification for many wicked choices. He is saying that he is unable to work with his own hands. He has developed his life so that all he knows, practically, is how to live off of others. To use others for his own benefit. This is what he has been doing to the Good Master for all of this time.

He is also unwilling to try. He is, at his core, a lazy man who is unwilling to earn a living without deceit. This is not a passive consequence of his life. This is the result of the way he has always desired to live. Unfortunately for this steward, by developing this talent for living off of people, and as a result of being relieved of his position, the steward is now faced with the proposition of starting back with nothing. He won't even have the recommendation from his last employer.

I cannot dig; to beg I am ashamed. (Luke 16:3b)

Until one faces where they are in life, they will be unable to make the changes that they desire. At this point in his life, if the steward were to live honestly, he would be in the position of a beggar. Since this would be his honest position in the world, there should be no shame in begging. There is no shame in honestly dealing with where one is in life. However, he openly states that he would be ashamed to beg. It is a good lesson to learn: that an honest life requires humility. The steward confesses himself unwilling.

The steward states that his shame would be in begging. Where is his shame for being kicked out of the Good Master's employ? Where is his shame for being found unjust? He sees no shame in either his immoral life, or in its public discovery. He has not submitted to the goodness of these judgments. Rather, while knowing that he needs provision, his shame is found in honest labor. Oh pride! Arrogance! He sees none of this as ungodly. It is the iniquity that is found in the nature of each man that blinds him from the truth.

Continuing, we have the internal fight raging on as he answers his own question:

I am resolved what to do, that, when I am put out of the stewardship, they may receive me into their houses. (Luke 16:4)

Whenever we try to answer the question "What shall I do?", it displays our perception of the problem. The steward is resolved to make sure that he has a place to go once he has been kicked out of the Master's house. This tells us that the steward's problem is that he has no place to go, not that he has been discovered as unjust. His problem is that the Master *thinks* he's unjust. He doesn't see it that way and he has no desire to attempt reconciliation.

He decides to act in a way that will increase his ability to continually live off of others. He plans to set his affairs in order so that he can continue living in the iniquity in which he thrived while he was in his Master's employ. To do this, he arranges a gathering of some of his Master's largest accounts.

So he called every one of his lord's debtors unto him, and said unto the first, How much owest thou unto my lord? And he said, An hundred measures of oil. And he said unto him, Take thy bill, and sit down quickly, and write fifty. Then said he to another, And how much owest thou? And he said, An hundred measures of wheat. And he said unto him, Take thy bill, and write fourscore. (Luke 16:5-7)

He has already been found unjust, so the steward's next action is to continue in the unjust behavior in a way that will profit him. This passage describes how he had wasted the Master's goods. According to the culture at the time, being placed into a stewardship over one's goods involved being a property manager. He rented out lands, made sure that fields were tilled, things of this nature. So, the oil and the wheat that was owed to the Master was the equivalent of rent. It was the price being charged to these families so that they could live, and prosper, on the rich man's land. During his time as steward, the unjust man had raised the taxes to an almost impossible amount. Thereby, making it almost impossible for the family to thrive on the land.

One may look at this scenario and say, "Where is the problem? The rich man is getting richer." This would seem to be what the steward was being paid for. However, this is not the case. The steward was taking care of the Good Master's land through unjust means. In other words, he was representing the Good Master to be an Unjust Master. The steward's actions presented the Master to the world as a greedy tyrant. This was against the nature of the Master. By doing so, the steward tarnished the Good Master's name.

The Master, the representation of God the Father in this parable, was in the perfect position to affect the people around him. He could encourage others and generate prosperity for those living on his lands. This has always been the heart of the Good Master: to use His wealth and established strength to allow others to work and prosper. In doing so, His goal was that they would come to know and love the Master for His goodness. This is why he had to dismiss the steward.

3

The steward's plan for self preservation deserves further attention:

So he called every one of his lord's debtors unto him, and said unto the first, How much owest thou unto my lord? And he said, An hundred measures of oil. And he said unto him, Take thy bill, and sit down quickly, and write fifty. Then said he to another, And how much owest thou? And he said, An hundred measures of wheat. And he said unto him, Take thy bill, and write fourscore. (Luke 16:5-7)

The picture being drawn here is as shady as it sounds. The unjust steward has set up a midnight meeting with the debtors. We should remember that they are in so much debt, not because of the cost of the Master's land, but because of how much the steward had been seeking for himself. This meeting has both the look and feel of being illegal. His wants the debtors to believe that he is using the last of his authority to do them a favor behind the Master's back. He wants them to feel indebted to him so that they might offer him shelter, once he has been removed from the Good Master's house. It is as if the steward is saying, "Here you go, the last thing I can do is make your life easier. Remember who has tried to help you in these trying times. The Master has caught on and won't allow me to help you anymore. You know me, though, I help those I can. Remember that."

What a liar! What an accuser! The steward had taken the protection and righteousness of the Good Master and twisted it so that it became an arrow against him. If the debtors had known the heart of the Master, they would have known the wretched act that was occurring before their eyes.

Jesus continues speaking in verse 8:
And the lord commended the unjust steward, because he had done wisely: for the children of this world are in their generation wiser than the children of light.

The Lord commended the unjust steward because he had done wisely. He had been acting out iniquity and unrighteousness. Yet the Lord states that the steward had done wisely because he passionately behaved in a way that would use his present condition to provide for a future necessity. He had behaved wisely for himself. This must not be confused with behaving wisely in the general sense. He was a man with a need. He saw an opportunity and satisfied that need to the best of his ability.

Herein lies the seemingly contradictory commendation. He behaved wisely for himself, therefore, wisdom must be acknowledged. However, as wise as it was for the steward to solve his immediate dilemma, the Lord is not commending the unjustness of the steward's heart. Nor is the Lord advocating that there is a time and a place for iniquity.

Jesus continues:
And I say unto you, Make to yourselves friends of the mammon of unrighteousness; that, when ye fail, they may receive you into everlasting habitations. (v9)

The unjust steward represents the lost individual who carries on with the affairs of the world. He represents the person that is taking care of himself. He is walking out the iniquity that is found in the heart of everyone. He has demonstrated that he has something that we, as born again individuals, lack. What could the lost possibly possess that those who are born of the spirit lack?

The lost have a debt that must be paid: the debt of sin. This is the biggest debt of all, and there is coming a day wherein each man's debt will be called into account. The lost have a very strong need that absolutely must be met. Passionately pursuing iniquity will not get anyone closer to relieving the burden of their sin. (Remember, our Lord was not commending the iniquity.) However, even if his chosen method of fixing his problem was doomed from the beginning, he was doing the two wisest things a lost man can do: he recognized his need and he passionately pursued a solution.

If we are covered by the Blood of the Lamb, our sins have been washed clean. We have no debt to pay because Jesus paid our debt in full on the Cross at Calvary! We will no longer have to give an account for our sins. He will recognize the nature of the Blood of His Son that covers us and He will know our names! How marvelous indeed!

However, here is the problem that our Lord is illuminating. If we aren't going to have to give an account for our sins, then where does our motivation come from? We will never again have the fear of death as a motivation. We no longer have an inherent dilemma that our life depends on solving. The problem that motivates all behavior in a lost individual has been solved for us.

There is something wise about the way that lost people will attempt to take care of themselves, even if the results are inevitably fruitless. This is something that the Lord is saying we must examine.

Then the steward said within himself, What shall I do? for my lord taketh away from me the stewardship: I cannot dig; to beg I am ashamed. (v3)

The steward is posing the question: "Now that I am to lose my stewardship, what am I to do?" He answers this question wisely, but out of iniquity. However, it is possible for us to answer this question in righteousness. There is a simple difference between iniquity and righteousness. The difference lies in *when* we ask: "What shall I do?"

Had the steward asked himself this question when the Master first gave him the stewardship (rather than to solve the problem of his impending fate), then he would have had an opportunity for righteousness. The steward's heart was full of iniquity, so this is not something that he would have been able to carry out. However we, as those who are saved, have been given the freedom to ask: "What is the Lord's heart that I should do?"

The Lord is reminding us that we have a race to run, so we need to decide now how we are to run it. The steward was an unjust man, but he behaved wisely. Will we who have been made just behave as wisely? Will we behave as if there is a need to be filled?   Will we remember to store for ourselves treasures in heaven?

The difference here must be underscored.   We have the option to store up treasures in heaven or not. The lost don't have an option but to try to solve the problem of their impending death. They must act, and they will do so wisely.   Since our life is assured, regardless of our behavior, then we must decide: What shall I do?

4

And the Pharisees also, who were covetous, heard all these things: and they derided him. And he said unto them, Ye are they which justify yourselves before men; but God knoweth your hearts: for that which is highly esteemed among men is abomination in the sight of God. (Luke 16:14-15)

This passage compares the reaction of the Pharisees with the heart of the unjust steward. They were wise in their ability to justify themselves among men, but they were unwilling to examine their own role before God. The steward's late night act of iniquity was as natural to him as swimming is to a fish. While unjust, he was being the steward that he knew how to be. He was very skilled in his iniquity and he was counting on it to cover his impending need. (Look at Jeremiah's description, in chapter 17, of the partridge trying to hatch an empty egg.)

...for that which is highly esteemed among men is abomination in the sight of God

It is this iniquity, the unrighteous fight for control, that is highly esteemed among men. However, it is an abomination to God. It will not fulfill the need that God knows the sinner has and it will never account for the debt that must be paid on Judgment Day. However, due to the iniquity that is in his heart, man will demand to use his own judgment, rather than submit to the will of God.

It is important to note that the idea of taking what you want from life is inseparable from the idea of taking from others that which does not belong to you. It is the demand from the heart of a thief. The only things that we can rightfully call our own are the things that we have been given by the Lord. This leaves only two choices: live our life by making manifest the gifts that the Lord has given us (diligently and faithfully using that which we are entrusted) or demanding to get the things that our hearts lust after. By definition, one does not lust after something that he already has, he lusts after something that is owned by someone else.

As stewards, if we were to recognize our stewardship, we would be recognizing the gift that had been given to us. Moreover, we would recognize that these gifts are ultimately intended for those around us, to whom we have the opportunity to minister. Our role is to provide them with the one thing that they need to prosper. In the parable, the steward was given stewardship over land. We have been given stewardship over something much more precious, and important, to the lives of the lost and dying. We are the bearers of the Gospel!

The unjust steward never recognized that his gift was the ability to bring life to those around him. He never realized that, while he was in the Good Master's house, all of his needs were provided for. He wanted to take the gift of the Master for himself, and in doing so, lost his own. He thought that he needed to build up wealth for himself, rather than building up the storehouse of the One providing for him. Had he known the Good Master's heart, had the steward seen the Good Master not as just *a* master, or the master of the debtors, but rather as *his* Master, then he would have been a *just* steward.

for the children of this world are in their generation wiser than the children of light.

The steward may have been unjust, but he was good at what he did. As discussed earlier, inflating the rent that the debtors owed and then adjusting it when it suited his own needs was the natural behavior of the steward. However, even though it was unjust behavior, it was labor. It might have been immoral labor, but it was labor nonetheless.

It is important that we not lose the value of diligent labor. The world knows the importance of passionate labor because they need it to survive. We need to remember the importance of passionate labor so that we may build up the kingdom of heaven.

The Lord has given labor to show us our own nature. He uses it to show a man the condition of his heart. For the lost, this provides evidence that the Holy Ghost can highlight during conviction. However, for the saved man, labor provides insight to the areas in one's life that the Lord is sanctifying. This is something we need to take seriously, if we are to be obedient to the command to "work out your salvation with fear and trembling" (Phil 2:12).

The more we are willing to put our hands to do the work the Good Master has called us to, the more we will be able to know *His* justness and *His* justification. For those who are born again, we can be assured that the more we walk in diligent labor, the more we will desire to know the Lord. Pressing into the heart of the Father, then, requires both faith and thanksgiving, as well as obedience and pursuit of the goals of the ministry that have been entrusted to us.

After much diligent working of the faith, the Apostle Paul exemplified that seeing the Goodness of the Father leads to a greater understanding of the wretchedness of our own heart. ("Oh wretched man that I am…" Romans 7:24). This, in turn, leads to an increasing need to cling to the heart of the Father so that we may be more like Him in the end.

He that is faithful in that which is least is faithful also in much: and he that is unjust in the least is unjust also in much. If therefore ye have not been faithful in the unrighteous mammon, who will commit to your trust the true riches? (Luke 16:10-11)

If we are unwilling to put our hands to labor faithfully in the insignificant tasks to provide the basic needs of life, then how can we be seen as trustworthy to receive the personal application of His Word? If we are not willing to be faithful with the tools given to us in the human (the day to day in which the world labors so diligently), then how could we be trusted with the tools to do the work needed in ministry?

The way in which we handle the financial affairs of this world can be used to show where one's heart truly lies. If you are willing to be faithful and become prosperous, what, then, is the goal of your labor? Is it, like that of the unjust steward, to find yourself to be wealthy? Or does your passion lie in line with the Good

Master, seeking to use his wealth to secure the lives of those around him? If we show that we treat the affairs of this world with the heart of the Father, then He has much to bless. After we demonstrate our faithfulness in the small areas of life, He will allow us to take part in matters He deems to be more important. We must remember that it is His work, not ours, to complete. We are just able to be partakers of the ministry with which he has entrusted us.

And if ye have not been faithful in that which is another man's, who shall give you that which is your own? (v12)

With this verse in mind, it is important to remember verse 3.

Then the steward said within himself, What shall I do? for my lord taketh away from me the stewardship: I cannot dig; to beg I am ashamed.

The steward realized that he had nothing. He realized, too late, that all the benefits he enjoyed belonged to the Good Master, and not himself. He had been treating everything as if it was his own. Now, since he has been stripped of the stewardship, he has nothing.

Not only was the steward left without anything to his name, he was also left without the ability to provide for himself. During his employ, he could only live off of the Good Master. After his removal, he found it necessary to put all of his efforts into living off of the debtors. He was still unable to make anything for himself.

As a man full of iniquity, it was impossible for him to have honestly earned anything in his life. In the same way, the lost man is unable to store up righteousness for himself.

And I say unto you, Make to yourselves friends of the mammon of unrighteousness; that, when ye fail, they may receive you into everlasting habitations. (v9)

No man can serve two masters. For either he will hate the one and love the other or else he will hold to one and despise the other. You cannot serve both God and mammon. (v13)

In one verse, we are being told to be familiar with the way the world uses money and the next verse says that we can't serve both God and mammon. The wonderful thing is this isn't contradictory. We are being told that mammon is not the problem. Money is important. However, it is even more important to be able to justly use money for the benefit of others.

The conflict that is being described is one that arises often in our fallen state. It points to the motivation and desires of our heart. How do we handle the internal conflict that arises when we lust after the same things as the world? The Lord is trying to teach us that a just steward will sacrifice his own lusts daily and identify the source of his desire: God or money. Jesus is using money to show us that, if we are unable to deal with the basic aspects of living in this world justly, then we will be unfit to be stewards of heavenly things. The unregenerate man can only deal with the affairs of life through iniquity. However, God uses a godly person's dealings with the corrupt world to give testimony of His own character. Those in this world are able to distinguish whether our behaviors are for our own benefit or in humble submission to the Lord.

It is a false assertion, however, that we must not desire to have anything if we are to be good stewards. This is a false humility. The truth is that our desires must first be in Him. He is a Good God and wants to give us the desires of our hearts (Psalms 37:4). The steward that loves his Master will simply be constantly aware that he is accountable to his Master for how he handles His affairs. This steward knows that all he has belongs to the Master first and that his behavior will reflect the nature of the Master to others. The godly steward will only want for himself that which the Lord wants to give him. He would see it as a treacherous act to take that which the Lord has for another. In other words, the godly steward knows that his needs are satisfied and that it is his role to bring life to others in the name of the Good Master.

In this passage, serving mammon is embodied by the motivation of providing for one's own personal gain. Serving God is, in essence, the motivation to ensure that others have the provision that the Master desires. This message that the Lord is giving is something that is being told on both the practical and spiritual level. The Lord has given so generously to us both the knowledge and experience of Him. While we will always have this bold access, it is now others who need to be covered by the Blood of the Lamb.

So it is that this conflict between lust and affection exists. The resolution comes down to a motivation of desires. Which is more important, to use the provision (either spiritual or practical) the way it is intended to be used, or to be kept for self? We cannot serve both God and our own lustful desire to possess.

5

And the Pharisees also, who were covetous, heard all these things: and they derided him. And he said unto them, Ye are they which justify yourselves before men; but God knoweth your hearts: for that which is highly esteemed among men is abomination in the sight of God. (v14-15)

This verse brings us out of the parable and back into Jesus' interactions with those around Him. The unjust man in the first part of the parable represents the Pharisees that are listening. They were the stewards of God's word and the only source the common man had for anything concerning God. However, they had grown arrogant. They loved their position and power more than they loved their God. During the telling of this parable, they began to make the same error, as the steward. The steward's glasses had been the wrong color. He saw his problem as the fact that he was getting fired, not that he was unjust. After hearing Jesus' words, the Pharisees were quickened about their sin before God. Instead of reacting in humility, they were quick to justify their positions in their hearts.

Had the unjust steward, or any one of the Pharisees, surrendered to being called unjust by the Master, then they would have cried out, saying, "Justify me! For you are the Good Master. I renounce my unjustness and beg to be given hospitality so that I might grow in your good ways!"

Such a humble repentance is the bending of one's will to the conviction from the Good Master. It is the only response that the Lord honors by destroying the iniquity in a man's heart. This response is the putting away of the inner fight of iniquity. Following that repentance He will wash us in the Blood of the Lamb and make us into new creatures. These new creatures have a different natural mindset than iniquity: the desire to please the Good Master.

The Lord is good in that He provides the lost with the opportunity to repent and be born again. His entire motivation when interacting with those who have not been made into a new creature is to provide an opportunity for His Blood to cover their sins. Every time that the Holy Ghost interacts with a lost man, it results in conviction of sins so that they may have an opportunity to repent. This parable is no exception. However, He is not only talking to the lost, but He has something to say to those that are *His,* as well.

Those that are lost cannot successfully handle the inherent problem of death. However, this does not change the fact that everything a lost man does is an attempt to deal with this problem. Working diligently at the inherent dilemma is part of the wisdom described earlier. Those who are born again no longer have this inherent dilemma. Since their motivation is clear, we have an important question to ask ourselves. What is the basis for our motivation?

Each new creature has experienced an incredible, life changing transformation. This transformation has satisfied every internal conflict, and provided us with an uninhibited access to know the Father more closely. However, we are still left in this old body. This means we are now given the decision of what it is that we will value and pursue. Will we press in, through obedience and submission, and seek to know Him more? Or will we go our own way? Phil 2:12 says:

Therefore, my beloved, as ye have always obeyed, not as in my presence only, but now much more in my absence, work out your own salvation with fear and trembling.

It is very important for us to obey the drive to seek out the heart of the Father. We cannot forget that our salvation is in Him. We need to walk out our salvation with fear and trembling. This means we need to, moment by moment, cling to the Lord with both our behavior and our affections. There are, tragically, many things in this world that separate us from Him, some more subtly than others. Peter tells us that if one does not diligently add to his faith, then he has forgotten that his sins have been forgiven (2 Peter 1:9). It is of supreme importance that we restore the foundation that the Lord, not any concept, is the source of all of our life.

The largest distraction from the Lord today takes the form of Christian values. The whole of the Gospel is that Jesus died to redeem sinners. The Gospel does not talk about Jesus requiring that we value and study the idea of redemption. The Gospel shows us the need for Jesus to redeem mankind.

When the stewards of His Gospel preach an understanding of the Gospel, rather than a transformation by the Gospel, they have ceased proclaiming God as He really is. By doing this, they begin to store up for themselves philosophies that appear to be godly, but are really validating their own position. While the steward might believe that he is preaching about God, he is, in reality, building the storehouse of his ego. Jesus came that we might know Him, not for us to get as many good ideas from Him as possible, then go our own way with them.

When the need of a Savior is debased into valuing a concept, or doctrine, of salvation, conversion becomes a framework for better living. After this compromise takes root, the experience of conviction and regeneration becomes less important. We are left with information to learn and integrate into our lives. This allows an individual to become a Christian without requiring repentance. Unfortunately, this describes a large portion of modern Christianity. This cannot be! If we can live up to an idea, we no longer need a real Savior.

A unique example of this misconception of modern Christianity lies in the Beatitudes.

Blessed are the poor in spirit: for theirs is the kingdom of heaven. Blessed are they that mourn: for they shall be comforted. Blessed are the meek: for they shall inherit the earth. Blessed are they which do hunger and thirst after righteousness: for they shall be filled. Blessed are the merciful: for they shall obtain mercy. Blessed are the poor in heart: for they shall see God. Blessed are the peacemakers: for they shall be called the children of God. Blessed are they which are persecuted for righteousness' sake: for theirs is the kingdom of heaven. (Matthew 5:3-10)

The error preached by the modern church is that Jesus is telling us to be meek, to mourn, etc. The modern church preaches this because it feeds the most basic human desire: to be able to live up to the righteous requirements of God. This is something that no one can possibly do.

Instead of telling us which types of values are Christian, Jesus is describing the type of blessing that is attributed to different character traits of the regenerated man. While these character traits will produce certain types of behaviors, the Lord tells us that He looks upon the heart. Actions can, in a spiritual sense, be fraudulent. They may not accurately describe one's nature. If one wants to be seen as honest, all he has to do is make sure others believe he is telling the truth. This does not mean that this person is honest, only that his immediate behavior is not a lie.

It is the interaction with our Savior that produces a meek character in us. When we no longer feel the need for our Savior, we are only able to learn *behaviors*. This will only allow us to *behave* meekly, something completely different from *being* meek. Therefore, while the actions attributed to these traits are important, the Lord is showing us *who* He will make us to be, not *how* He wants us to behave. These character traits are only humanly possible if they are the result of a personal interaction with the Lord. We should not seek to be meek or poor in heart, but rather, to seek the Lord. Through communion with our Savior, we will be able to affect others as good stewards.

As Jesus was describing in the parable of the wise but unjust steward, the lost have an inherent motivation: prevent death, both physical and eternal. Those who are saved have had the problem of death taken away and have been given the opportunity to seek out the Lord's heart. His motivation can be our own. However, this is only possible if our daily walk is focused on remembering, and being thankful, for what He did for us, personally (2 Peter 1:8-9). As we focus on Him, He will show us the desires that He has for us and those around us. Then, out of our motivation to please the Father, He will give us the characteristics needed to succeed in the task of pleasing Him.

However, if our only goal is to experience and understand things for ourselves, then we will have lost the only Godly motivation available to us. It is this desire to have, rather than to please Him, that keeps us from experiencing God's redemption and justification. We want to have godly knowledge so that we can then make our own judgments from it. This only allows us to fill our life with an understanding of the *ideas* of redemption and justification. Then all we have left is the struggle to live up to God's ideals, when we're supposed to be changed into them.

Two Natures

Wicked Christianity

In the first two epistles of John two words are used over and over, the words *they* and *ye,* and they designate two wholly separate worlds. *They* refers to the men and women of Adam's fallen world; *ye* refers to the chosen ones who have left all to follow Christ. The apostle does not genuflect to the little god *Tolerance* (the worship of which has become in America a kind of secondary surface religion); he is bluntly intolerant. He knows that tolerance may be merely another name for indifference. It takes a vigorous faith to accept the teaching of the man John. It is so much easier to blur the lines of separation and so offend no one. Pious generalities and the use of *we* to mean both Christians and unbelievers is much safer. The fatherhood of God can be stretched to include everyone from Jack the Ripper to Daniel the Prophet. Thus no one is offended and everyone feels quite snug and ready for heaven. But the man who laid his ear on Jesus' breast was not so easily deceived. He drew a line to divide the race of men into two camps, to separate the saved from the lost, those who shall rise to eternal reward from them that shall sink into final despair. On one side are *they* that know not God; on the other *ye* (or with a change in person, *we*), and between the two is a moral gulf too wide for any man to cross. Here is the way John states it:

"*Ye are of God, little children, and have overcome them: because greater is he that is in you, than he that is in the world. They are of the world: therefore speak they of the world, and the world heareth them. We are of God: he that knoweth God heareth us; he that is not of God heareth not us. Hereby we know the spirit of truth and the spirit of error*" (I John 4:4-6)

Such language as this is too plain to confuse anyone who honestly wants to know the truth. Our problem is not one of understanding, I repeat, but of faith and obedience. The question is not a theological one, What does this teach? It is a moral one, Am I willing to accept this and abide by its consequences? Can I endure the cold stare? Have I the courage to stand up to the slashing attack of the "liberal"? Dare I invite the hate of men who will be affronted by my attitude? Have I independence of mind sufficient to challenge the opinions of popular religion and go along with an apostle? Or briefly, can I bring myself to take up the cross with its blood and its reproach?

- A. W. Tozer (God's Pursuit of Man)

"Be ye doers of the Word and not hearers only, deceiving your own selves. For if any be a hearer of the Word, and not a doer, he is like unto a man beholding his natural face in a glass. For he beholdeth himself and goeth his way and straightway forgetteth what manner of man he was." James 1:22

If there is one thing that separates Christianity from other religions, it is the intimate relationship between God and His believers. This relationship can be seen when God uses His Word as a mirror to show each reader his true nature and eternal standing. It is important to understand the nature of this interaction with the Word. When the Word of God is preached, it is neither for the purpose of refining behavior nor for personal enrichment. God has designed His Word so that, when it is preached, it highlights the nature of the hearer. It shows the hearer both who God is and the hearer's position before Him. He does not do this in order to merely highlight our inadequacies. It is the deep desire of our God that all men come to salvation. In His sovereignty, God uses His Word to show us who we are so that we can see our need for this offered salvation.

"As it is written, There is none righteous, no, not one: There is none that understandeth, there is none that seeketh after God. They are all gone out of the way, they are together become unprofitable; there is none that doeth good, no, not one. Their throat is an open sepulchre; with their tongues they have used deceit; the poison of asps is under their lips: Whose mouth is full of cursing and bitterness: Their feet are swift to shed blood: Destruction and misery are in their ways: And the way of peace have they not known: There is no fear of God before their eyes." (Romans 3:10-18)

In Romans 3, Paul is describing the nature of the lost person. This describes each person's state before encountering the

Gospel. Each can only operate off of the basic law of their nature: sin. Mercifully, God wrote His laws on each heart in the form of our conscience. However, we believe that we are the source of this moral code because we are able to discern between good and evil. The most that anyone living under the Law can do is eschew evil and embrace good. We end up living a life that meets our moral standards. We create an image of ourselves based on our perceived level of moral discernment. In essence, since we believe that we can choose good, then we believe that there is something good in us.

This is a fallacy, however because our problem does not lie in our choices, but in our nature. According to God's Word, nobody, even if they are spiritual and moral, wants to know God's true nature. He is fundamentally different and contrary to us in every way. Instead, we are looking for a god that fits our understanding of god. We are looking for a god that will forgive our sins and praise our good deeds. Like the rich young ruler, each lost man is looking for a good teacher to help him on his personal spiritual path. We want to know a god that enriches our lives the way we believe our lives need to be enriched. However, we are not looking for a god who sees us the way God really looks at us, which is:

They are together become unprofitable; there is none that doeth good, no, not one. Their throat is an open sepulchre (v12-13)

This means their throat is the doorway into a grave.

With their tongues they have used deceit; the poison of asps is under their lips: Whose mouth is full of cursing and bitterness: Their feet are swift to shed blood. (v13-15)

Remember, Jesus said that if someone has had unjust anger in their heart, they have committed murder (Matt. 5:21). This was not modifying the original commandment, but returning it to its original design. It is originally written that way in Leviticus (Leviticus 19:18). Unfortunately, due to our sinful nature, we focused on the "Thou shalt not" so that we could know what technical external standard was required. We became familiar with what we *weren't* supposed to do and conveniently left out how He wanted us to be. The Law was always designed to show us our nature. He provided the Laws of "thou shalt not" to show us that without God's intervention, those trespasses were natural to us.

Therefore by the deeds of the law there shall no flesh be justified in his sight: for by the law is *the knowledge of sin.* (v20)

While we need the Law to highlight who we are, it is not possible for the Law to save us. Life does not come from this Law; it can only show us the need for life. The Law can only highlight the death that is there. The death being shown is an active form of death. We're not corpses lying around. We are actively doing things. We are actively using deceit, being full of cursing, bitterness, and the murderous intentions. Our entire nature is constantly battling the Gospel. Our death means we are at war with God's work in our lives.

It is important to remember that the Law is a fundamental aspect of the Gospel. However, we must make sure that we are using it for the purpose intended. The Law tells us what it is that we are not allowed to do. This has the tendency to make us angry. There is no life that can come from "thou shalt not kill." The only result possible from obeying the commandment is a lack of murdered people. The entire end product of this Law is a lack of something, a negative space where a behavior would have been. There is nowhere to go from there. This defines the preserving nature of the Law. It is there to prevent the behavior that would produce major negative consequences. We need to be preserved by the Law because no life can come from our nature, only death.

Therefore by the deeds of the law there shall no flesh be justified in his sight: for by the law is the knowledge of sin. But now the righteousness of God without the law is manifested, being witnessed by the law and the prophets; Even the righteousness of God which is by faith of Jesus Christ unto all and upon all them that believe: for there is no difference: For all have sinned, and come short of the glory of God. (Romans 3:20-23)

And as it is appointed unto men once to die, but after this the judgment: So Christ was once offered to bear the sins of many; and unto them that look for him shall he appear the second time without sin unto salvation. (Hebrews 9:27-28)

When we are born, we arrive in a fallen world with a sinful nature. We will walk out our nature in all of its wickedness until our time of judgment. However, because of the work that Jesus did on the Cross, we are given the opportunity to be judged, with His judgment, during our lifetime. Our own judgment will come the moment we die. However, because Jesus was judged before us, He has provided a way for us to be judged with Him, so that when we reach the appointed time of our own judgment, we will be seen as holy as He is holy.

There is a moment in each person's life when the Law, which is written on each heart, is met with the preaching of the Word of God. During this moment, the Holy Spirit reveals the wickedness of a person's nature in contrast to the nature of our Savior. This is the point of conviction. It is the intimate moment where God interacts with a person. Each of the sins brought before the person at this time are only used as evidence of their nature. The implications of this are far reaching. It means that hell is not an "eternal penitentiary" for bad behavior, but rather our natural destination.

What shall we say then? Shall we continue in sin, that grace may abound? God forbid. How shall we, that are dead to sin, live any longer therein? Know ye not, that so many of us as were baptized into Jesus Christ were baptized into his death? Therefore we are buried with him by baptism into death: that like as Christ was raised up from the dead by the glory of the Father, even so we also should walk in newness of life. For if we have been planted together in the likeness of his death, we shall be also in the likeness of his resurrection: Knowing this, that our old man is crucified with him, that the body of sin might be destroyed, that henceforth we should not serve sin. For he that is dead is freed from sin. (Romans 6:1-7)

The question then becomes: how will the individual respond? The Bible makes it clear that belief is the requirement for salvation. The first evidence of this belief is repentance: a turning away from our life to the life of Jesus. This interaction splits humanity into two categories: those with their old natures crucified (the saved), and those who refused to repent (the lost).

It is important to not read too quickly through Romans 6. For the saved, there is satisfaction in reading that we are living in Christ. However, the existence of our life in Christ is dependent on the death of our nature *in this life*. We like to jump over to the "life in Christ," however before that can be a reality in our life, everything about our life needs to be crucified with Him on the cross. When this happens, our nature, along with all of our requirements to deal with the Law, is crucified with Him. The old nature needed to die so that we could move on to righteousness through a new nature. This new nature does not need the old Law, but is now bound by the new Law of Liberty. The born-again person no longer has a dead nature, but a new living nature. As a result, our Savior expects us to live with our new life, not simply re-create an old death.

Knowing that Christ being raised from the dead dieth no more; death hath no more dominion over him. For in that he died, he died unto sin once: but in that he liveth, he liveth unto God. (v9-10)

This verse means that we're in Him. He rose, not to die anymore. That means He's given us a nature that is free from death. This is why the lost have the lust of the mind and the desires of the mind. We once did, but we don't anymore. We can only remember having them. That means all we can have is the vanity of the mind, the memory of the old fruits of death, now unattainable in life. We can refuse to move on in the new law; however this cannot bring spiritual death again. Our death is gone. This does not mean that the believer will automatically prosper (spiritually) simply because he cannot die (spiritually). It is now the responsibility of the believer to passionately live out the life that he has been given.

Likewise reckon ye also yourselves to be dead indeed unto sin, but alive unto God through Jesus Christ our Lord. Let not sin therefore reign in your mortal body, that ye should obey it in the lusts thereof. Neither yield ye your members as instruments of unrighteousness unto sin: but yield yourselves unto God, as those that are alive from the dead, and your members as instruments of righteousness unto God. For sin shall not have dominion over you: for ye are not under the law, but under grace. What then? shall we sin, because we are not under the law, but under grace? God forbid. Know ye not, that to whom ye yield yourselves servants to obey, his servants ye are to whom ye obey; whether of sin unto death, or of obedience unto righteousness? (Romans 6:11-16)

It is extremely important for the believer to remember that he had nothing to do with his own salvation. If this fact gets ignored, then it is possible for the believer to be satisfied with the base level of spiritual morality that is attainable to a lost man. When a man was lost, he was under the law. He was forced to deal with life in under the terms of morality. Still, sin reigned in his body, even when he was obeying the law. He could have been the most moral person on the face of the earth, and the most devout Christian, yet, if he had not been put to death on the Cross with Jesus, all of his obedience meant death.

If we were to carry the mindset of morality into our new life in Christ, we may believe that our newly attained freedom is designed to make the moral obligations easier. Paul is saying that this is not true. If one is obedient to the Law, he is under death. Death is the only result of being a moral person. There is no opportunity for life if a person's goodness is based on a mere lack of sin. Our moral obligations died with our old man. The new life in Christ is not bound by the need to "not die." Death is no longer a concern. As such, we are not bound to decreasing sin, but to increasing godly affection. We are bound to life and required to live.

Know ye not, that to whom ye yield yourselves servants to obey, his servants ye are to whom ye obey; whether of sin unto death, or of obedience unto righteousness? (v16)

It is this duality of direction that differentiates the born again believer from his lost counterpart. All men, regardless of their position before God, are servants. This is by design. Man's fallen nature is, at it's essence, man demanding to be his own master, even when the consequences for this are death. As a measure of preservation, God provided moral law. The law decrees "Thou shalt not." This limited the temporal consequences from our service of death. However, the law of liberty decrees "Thou shalt," Following the law of liberty requires action. If we are adept at saying, "I won't," there is no way for us to live a godly life.

The "I won't" underneath the Law was important, in that it preserved us, keeping at bay the consequences of sin. The law and morality both dictate that we ought not to walk out our fallen nature. However, under the law of liberty, refusing to walk out our nature is to deny the work that God has done in our life. We will be unable to grow in Christ if we are unwilling to obey the demands of our new nature. We will never diligently add to the faith that cost such a high price.

As we begin to walk in our new nature, this precludes our ability to sin. It would be impossible to love our neighbor and kill him at the same time. Walking in godly love precludes murder. Therefore, there is no issue of sin while following in the nature that we've been given in Christ. (Galatians 5:16) However, if we return to the idea of simply limiting behavior, we will have forgotten who we are.

Being then made free from sin, ye became the servants of righteousness. I speak after the manner of men because of the infirmity of your flesh: for as ye have yielded your members servants to uncleanness and to iniquity unto iniquity; even so now yield your members servants to righteousness unto holiness. For when ye were the servants of sin, ye were free from righteousness. (v18-20)

This last statement should resound with anyone who has worked within the field of counseling. It is not easy to help someone escape the bonds of whatever is holding them back and allow them to simply live and enjoy life. We have this fundamental desire to run away from the responsibility of living. We have a fundamental unwillingness to deal with the fact that we exist. It is not easy to put our choices out there,: to compare it with scripture and see who you really are. Without the Holy Ghost operating within our life, this is a spiritually impossible act. While we were dead, we were relieved of our responsibility to live.

The lost man is a servant of sin and the religion of morality was as close as one could get to God. The lost man does not have to worry about loving his neighbor as long as he doesn't murder him. However, once we have been given new life, we are not allowed to continue under this spiritual disconnect. The completed law is to love the Lord your God with all your heart, soul, mind and strength and love your neighbor as yourself. (Matt. 22:37-40) This law speaks to a great deal more than do not kill, steal, or murder. If one is born again, he has the ability to do this because God has given him a new nature. The born again man would have to against his nature to go back into sin. This is why all of the directives for the Christian life in the New Testament are not new Laws, but a description of the design of the new nature. We are not required to love in order to gain heaven. Rather, we are told to be obedient to His Word because it tells us who He has made us to be.

If there is one idea that defines the life of a believer, it is *obedience*. From the first act of obedience during salvation (repentance and belief) to the daily submission to the Word that encompasses the Christian walk, obedience to God's Word is the basic method Christians use to walk out their faith. Unlike other religions, this obedience is not an attempt to earn heaven or an attempt to earn God's favor. Christians obey out of a heartfelt devotion to the God that bestowed His favor on those that are supremely aware of their unworthiness (John 14:15).

It is this awareness that sets the obedience of a believer apart from mere religion. When the Word is preached, the Holy Ghost interacts with the hearer on a personal level. During this interaction, the Holy Ghost compares the nature of the individual to the Word that has been preached. This is enough to convince man of his wicked condition. The combined knowledge of their wicked condition and Christ's sacrifice produces a deep devotion that is displayed through obedience. However, when someone begins to forget the Holy Ghost's revelation of their nature, they forget about their own wickedness and lose the inner drive towards obedience. In short, when someone forgets about their own nature they will lose the motivation to obey God's Word. When this happens, James is telling us that a Christian no longer believes the faith that they claim.

But whoso looketh into the perfect law of liberty, and continueth therein. He being not a forgetful hearer, but a doer of the work, this man shall be blessed in his deed. (James 1:25)

The relationship between regeneration and obedience is fundamental to a true Christian's walk. In fact, if obedience to God's Word was not present in a person's life, their regeneration should be highly suspect. It is with this understanding that James begins to describe the law of liberty. This is an unusual phrase that seems, on its surface, to be a contradiction in terms. The general understanding of spiritual liberty entails being set free from subjection to the law. Yet, this phrase signifies that Christians are bound by freedom. The "law of liberty" perfectly describes the position in which a believer stands through regeneration. How is it that the believer is bound by his lack of boundaries?

Inherently, being under the law of liberty is different from being under the Law. A man underneath the law of liberty never forgets the characteristics of his old nature. It is the moment of conversion that draws a distinction between the two types of people hearing the Word: those who have been redeemed and those in need of redemption. We can see the outline of the spiritual life of man through the life that Jesus lived. He lived His life as a testimony to what the life of the believer is in the big picture. He lived, He walked in His nature, He was judged (albeit for our sins, not his), and then He was rose again. That is the walk of the believer. We walk in our nature before we are judged, and then we're judged. However, how we respond to that judging will determine whether the Lord gets glory in our salvation or in our eternal punishment.

Unfortunately, modern Christianity has failed to understand what is being judged. We want to believe that it is our behavior that is on trial. Our behavior is simply the evidence of our *nature* presented at the judgment. The Gospel judges our fallen and unrighteous nature. It is who we are that is being judged, not what we do. We require a new birth in order to truly live. Once Christ paid the penalty for our sins, He made the way so that those who were willing to repent and believe would find the God that searched for them.

Nee, Watchman. *Sit, Walk, Stand.* (1977) Tyndale Publishing House.

Tozer, A. W., *God's Pursuit of Man.* (2011) Authentic Lifestyle. 3rd Revised Edition

King James Bible

www.ingramcontent.com/pod-product-compliance
Lightning Source LLC
Chambersburg PA
CBHW031327040426
42443CB00005B/245